MINA SOUNDAR

Heartbreak Karma

One mantra to find your true love

To the heartbroken by love, know that this too shall pass and that sunnier days are just around the corner if you are just a little bit braver enough to open your heart and mind.

"I seem to have loved you in numberless forms, numberless times, in life after life, in age after age forever."

– Rabindranath Tagore

Contents

Preface

Love is one of the most influential and transformative forces in our lives, capable of bringing us immense joy, happiness, and deep pain and heartbreak. When experiencing heartbreak, my entire world turned upside down, and I felt alone and uncertain about the future.

Yet, as painful as heartbreak can be, it also catalyzes growth, transformation, and spiritual awakening. Amid my pain and suffering, I asked more profound questions about the nature of love, my life's purpose, and spirituality's role in my healing and growth.

In this book, I will explore the intersection of heartbreak and spirituality and how the wisdom of spiritual traditions and practices has helped me navigate the challenges of love and heartbreak. We will delve into the mysteries of the Universe, from the vastness of space to the secrets of the heart, and discover how these mysteries can provide comfort, healing, and inspiration in times of pain and struggle.

Drawing on insights from ancient spiritual traditions, including mindfulness, meditation, prayer, mysticism, and physics, we will explore practical tools and techniques for healing our hearts and cultivating deeper connections to ourselves, others, and the Universe. Whether you are going through a difficult breakup, struggling with the pain of unrequited love, or simply seeking greater meaning and purpose, this book is for you.

Together, let us explore the journey of heartbreak and spiritual awakening and discover the wisdom, beauty, and grace that lie at the heart of this profound and transformative experience.

Introduction

The most painful thing is losing yourself in the process of loving someone too much and forgetting that you are special too.
  Ernest Hemingway

As I sat alone in my room, tears streaming down my face, I couldn't help but wonder what was wrong with me. Why couldn't I find someone who loved me for who I was? Whenever I opened up to someone, I was hurt and alone.

I felt lost and directionless like I was wandering through life without purpose. All my dreams and plans for the future seemed meaningless without someone to share them with. The pain of rejection and heartbreak weighed heavily on my chest, making breathing hard.

I questioned my worth and wondered if my destiny was to be alone forever. I sometimes envied those around me who seemed to have had no problems finding their partners effortlessly, wondering why it was so difficult for me.

Despite my best efforts to move on and start anew, the memories of past relationships and the pain of heartbreak lingered, leaving me feeling stuck and helpless. My heart shattered into a million pieces, and I had no idea how to put it back together again.

I have always believed that someone is out there for everyone, a soul mate who completes us and makes us whole. But for me, the search for love was a long and arduous journey filled with heartbreak and disappointment.

I started my search for love in India, my home country, where arranged marriages are still prevalent. Despite several attempts, none of the matches felt right, and I couldn't imagine spending my life with any of them. I then moved to Australia for higher education, hoping that a change of scenery would bring me luck in love. However, I faced similar challenges and found myself in relationships that never worked out.

My work and my search then took me to the United States, where I thought I would find more opportunities to meet people and find my soul mate. However, even after several relationships, I was still left feeling unfulfilled and alone.

It wasn't until I arrived in Europe that things finally began to change. Though I was doing great in my career, it was still hurting. It was during this dark and challenging time that I turned to spirituality for solace and guidance, seeking to find meaning and purpose in my suffering and finding what I was looking for - I met my soul mate, someone who understood me on a deep level and whom I could see myself spending the rest of my life with.

Looking back, my journey of finding love has so many valuable lessons. Each experience taught me more about myself and what I wanted in a partner. And while the trip was difficult, it ultimately led me to the person meant for me.

I am grateful for the heartbreak and disappointment that led me to where I am today. I am more confident in myself and my ability to recognize a healthy and fulfilling relationship. And most importantly, I am happy and content with the knowledge that I have found my soul mate.

I

Healing the broken heart

One

My Search for Love

N ever allow someone to be your priority while allowing yourself to be your option.
Mark Twain

Melbourne, Australia

It was time. I finally had to decide to end the more than five years of futile relationship with my boyfriend. What else should I do? It became painfully apparent that we were incompatible, and he preferred to live securely with his parents. Overprotected and too scared to live life.

It did not quite match my personality – outgoing, adventurous, happy-go-lucky traveler. You would think I might have known this already. But, strangely enough, I did not. Didn't someone wise say, "Hindsight 20-20?"

I still remember the day I broke up with him. t was a bright and sunny day, but the sun's warmth did nothing to ease the coldness in my heart. Sitting across from him in a coffee shop, I could feel my hands trembling and my heart racing.

We had been together for five long years, but things had started to fall apart over the last few months – slowly building up over the years. What did not help was my upcoming six-month assignment in New Zealand. But it was this assignment that threw light on the problem. During these months, he had never made an effort to come and visit me even once. I was the only person flying to and for a couple of times to see him in Australia. He was too scared to fly; his parents did not allow him. Even though he still "loved" me, the disagreements and arguments had become more frequent, and the love and affection I felt for him once seemed to have vanished.

I knew that it was time to end things, but the thought of breaking his heart and losing the person who had been my companion and confidante for so long was almost unbearable. My mind raced with questions and doubts as I gathered the courage to say the words.

What if I was making a mistake? What if I never found someone who loved me as much as he did? What if I am to be alone forever?

My resolve wavered as I looked into his eyes and saw the pain and confusion on his face. But deep down, I knew that we were no longer suitable for each other and that the only way to move forward was to let go.

The rest of that day went by as a blur of tears and heartache. The once familiar places and things that had once brought me comfort and joy now seemed empty and hollow. The future stretched like an endless abyss, and I had no idea where to turn.

* * *

USA

You can imagine my relief and happiness when I received a new job offer to go on a new adventure overseas to Texas. In Dallas, I met my new boyfriend.

It was all so beautiful at first, but the incompatibility soon started to show. This time, it is because I am not a goth nor a fan of a role-playing group, and, indeed, I wouldn't say I liked that most of my boyfriend's friends were girls. Though I am not jealous or insecure, I felt alarm bells ring in my head. I knew that in my heart, I would not be happy and could not stay. Still, it was not an easy move. Regrets, fear, and sadness all engulfed me, and lo and behold, I watched my future again in all its emptiness. Devastated and depressed – I thought with much despair - Whatever should become of me now? My relationships seem not to work out well at all.

***

Europe, here I come!

Thanks to my lucky stars, I received a new job offer from Europe. Just the break I had been praying for.

While focused on work in my new country of residence, I met a new boyfriend - divorced with a grown-up daughter. Again, the earlier pattern followed – the relationship was great at first, but soon the key differences popped up like priorities – I wanted to start a family, on the other hand, he was getting ready for retirement, as he has already been there done that.

Unhappiness, confusion, and restlessness start to bubble up. I became desperate to find a soul mate with whom I could have a harmonious relationship and row together in the same direction.

I am a slow learner. However, I have learned my lessons. I knew what did not work for me. I made progress by eliminating all the characters and features I did NOT want in my life companion, so through all the heartache, I was progressing in my search for love. Of course, I understood by now that it is OK to have different interests and differences of opinion. Still, I craved a caring relationship founded on true love and affection and wanted similar things in life on the most fundamental aspects, which were close to my heart.

That's when I came across the method of praying and chanting as a solution for finding one's life partner. I decided to try this method and not only try in passing but to give it my best. No sitting on the fence, no halfheartedness. I liked this method of not having to approach anyone else but going directly to the vast Universal Force to explain my situation and ask for what I wished.

Almost four months after practicing this one mantra, day and night, I met my husband, the one I had been searching for all my life.

In this book, I want to share my thought process and perspectives I adopted when experiencing breakups and how these new perspectives helped me accept the pain in my heart. I also share the simple steps I undertook to find my partner eventually through prayer and mantra chanting. The steps are simple but very effective and easy for someone to follow.

There are two main parts to this book.

The first part introduces several perspectives and ideas for you to consider, which could be helpful in your healing process. You do not necessarily have to read the chapters in order. Sometimes, a fragment of an idea in one of the chapters could be sufficient to comfort or provide strength and set you on a path where you find your way out of heart pain.

The second part is about renewing hope after healing and how to find your soulmate if that is what you want.

If at least one reader can find hope and comfort in the contents and is inspired to try the steps I undertook and find the love of their life, then this book's purpose is fulfilled.

Two

The Big Picture

Our sorrows and wounds are healed only when we touch them
with compassion.
   Gautama Buddha

When I was heartbroken and despairing, I found stepping back from myself and drawing my attention to the world around me helpful. Looking beyond my heartbreak allowed my mind some breathing space and time to pause what it was experiencing at that moment, which it did not want to – excruciating pain.

And when I turned my attention to something wondrous and awe-inspiring, I forgot myself for some time, even for a split second. I was immersed in a different world, oblivious to the immediate painful circumstance. Of course, there were many times when I thought– but right now, nothing wondrous, nothing awe-inspiring, nothing can make me take notice, nothing I care for.

True.

At this moment, it would appear so. But nothing in this world stays the same. For better or worse, that is the law of nature.

Hence, I pondered over how it appeared as if my life was played with, as it were, by the Hand of God. I turned my attention to this thought – my life, my family, this earth, our Universe, it all appeared to me like it's God's playground – I would like to do something and plan for it, but sometimes what happens is something different – quite contrary to my plans. Why does God play so with me?

God's playground

This idea of "God's playground" can be interpreted in various ways, depending on one's spiritual or philosophical beliefs. However, one possible way to understand this concept in the context of heartbreak is to view it as a more extensive, interconnected web of experiences and relationships orchestrated by a higher power or universal Consciousness.

From this perspective, I considered that the pain and heartbreak I was experiencing in love was a part of a larger pattern or purpose, even if I could not fully understand it in the present moment. I felt just like a child who did not understand the meaning of a playground or the rules of a game at first but gradually learned through experience and guidance; likewise, I, too, can grow and learn from my experiences of heartbreak.

One way I approached my heartbreak as part of "God's playground" is that I cultivated a sense of surrender and trusted in unfolding my life's experiences. It is easier said than done! It involved letting go of the need to control or predict my future, focusing on the present moment, and learning lessons from my pain.

It can also involve seeking guidance and support from spiritual practices or communities, such as prayer, meditation, or counseling. By connecting with others who share our struggles and seeking wisdom from higher sources, we can find comfort and guidance as we navigate the ups and downs of love and life.

Ultimately, "God's playground" is a deeply personal and subjective concept with different meanings and interpretations for other individuals. However, by approaching my heartbreak with openness, curiosity, and a willingness to learn and grow, I could find more profound meaning and purpose in my struggles and ultimately emerge more robust and resilient.

Big Space, Universes, and Galaxies

Now that we have looked at God's playground, the stage where all this, including my heartbreak, unfolded is in this real or surreal existing space. The space where we are born, live, hope, dream, and aspire. Heartbreak happens in the sacred spaces of our hearts. The great ample vast space outside is also inside us. As above, so below.

The great medical pioneer, Paracelsus, said, "Man is a microcosm, or a little world because he is an extract from all the stars and planets of the whole firmament, from the earth and the elements; and so he is their quintessence."

I found comfort in the vastness of space, the galaxies, and the Universe. Below are the reasons why I find space comforting.

Perspective: When going through my heartbreak, I easily got caught up in my pain and quickly lost perspective on the bigger picture. Looking up at the night sky and contemplating the vastness of space and the extensiveness and complexity of the Universe helped me regain a sense of perspective and realize that my problems are just a tiny part of a much larger universe. It helped me see my situation differently, feel less overwhelmed by my emotions, and gain a more objective and balanced perspective, reducing my emotions' intensity.

Resilience: The Universe is full of examples of strength and perseverance. From stars that survive despite incredible pressure and temperature to galaxies that continue to evolve despite countless obstacles, the Universe is a testament to the power of resilience. By contemplating these examples of stability, I was able to draw strength and inspiration for my journey of healing and growth.

Mystery: The Universe is full of mystery and wonder, and contemplating its mysteries has been helpful to shift my focus away from my pain and onto something more extensive and awe-inspiring. It provided comfort and a reminder that there is more to life than my struggles.

Beauty: the Universe is full of beauty and wonder, from the majesty of spiral galaxies to the intricacy of the smallest particles. By contemplating the beauty of the Universe, I could find solace and comfort in something larger than myself and reconnect with the joy and wonder at the heart of life.

Timelessness: Space is vast and timeless; contemplating its immensity has been helpful for me to remember that my pain and suffering are temporary. Even though I feel like my heartbreak will never end, the Universe has been around for billions of years and will continue to exist long after I am gone. It provides a sense of perspective and helps me remember that my current struggles are just a tiny part of our more extensive journey through life.

Connection: Finally, contemplating the vastness of space helped me feel a sense of connection to something larger than myself. We are all part of the same Universe, and we share our struggles with countless others who have come before us and will come after us. It can help us feel less alone in our pain and provide a sense of comfort and connection to others who are going through similar struggles.

The vastness of space and the galaxies can comfort someone suffering from a broken heart through love by providing perspective, resilience, mystery, beauty, timelessness, and connection. By contemplating the wonders of the Universe and by connecting with the majesty and mystery of the Universe, we can find solace, inspiration, and comfort in something larger than ourselves, healing our hearts and spirits by remembering that our struggles are just a tiny part of our more significant journey through life.

Dark Matter and Black Holes

When one door closes, another opens; but we often look so long and regretfully upon the closed door that we do not see the one that has opened for us.

   Alexander Graham Bell

Dark matter and black holes are fascinating and mysterious concepts in astrophysics, but they may not seem immediately relevant to matters of the heart. However, we can draw some interesting parallels between these astronomical phenomena and the human experience of heartbreak.

First, let us consider the dark matter. Scientists estimate that dark matter makes up about 85% of the matter in the Universe. Still, we cannot directly observe it because it does not interact with light or other forms of electromagnetic radiation. We can only detect its presence through its gravitational effects on visible matter. Similarly, the emotional pain of heartbreak can be difficult to observe or quantify directly, but we can feel its effects throughout life.

Now let us turn to black holes. These are regions of spacetime where the gravitational pull is so strong that nothing, not even light, can escape. They form from the collapse of a massive star. In the aftermath of heartbreak, it can feel like we are being pulled into a dark, bottomless pit, unable to escape the gravitational pull of our pain and sadness.

So, were these concepts helpful for me when I was dealing with heartbreak? Again, I was pondering over the resilience and adaptability of the Universe in the face of these seemingly insurmountable challenges. Despite the pervasive presence of dark matter and the intense gravitational pull of black holes, the Universe continues to expand and evolve. Similarly, even in the depths of heartbreak, I should find the strength to persevere and move forward with my life.

Additionally, the vastness and mystery of the cosmos remind me again that my struggles are just a tiny part of a much larger picture. I lost perspective and felt easily overwhelmed when focusing too narrowly on my pain. Looking up at the stars and contemplating the mysteries of the Universe helped me regain a sense of awe and wonder and reminded me that there is much more to life than my individual experiences.

Finding meaning and solace in heartbreak is a profoundly personal journey; there is no one-size-fits-all answer. However, drawing on the insights and wisdom of different fields, including astrophysics and spirituality, can help us broaden our perspective and find the strength to heal and move forward.

Our Planet Earth

The weak can never forgive. Forgiveness is the attribute of the strong.
  Mahatma Gandhi

Similarly, contemplating our dear Mother Earth can be helpful and supportive for a person suffering from the restlessness of a broken heart through love in several ways. I have listed below how Mother Earth was helpful to me.

Nature's Healing Power: When I spend time in nature, whether walking in the park, hiking in the woods, or simply sitting in a garden, I feel a calming and healing effect on my mind and body. Research indicates that spending time in nature can reduce stress, improve mood, and boost overall well-being.

Grounding and Connecting: When I experienced heartbreak, I often felt disconnected from myself and the world around me. However, spending time in nature helped me feel more grounded and connected to the earth and the natural world, providing stability and security.

Time for Reflection and Self-Care: Being in nature can also provide a space for reflection and self-care. Away from the distractions of technology and everyday life, I took the time to process my emotions, journal, and be with my thoughts and feelings. It was a powerful way for me to gain clarity and insight into my situation and to practice self-compassion and self-care.

Symbolism and Metaphor: Nature is full of symbolism and metaphor, which helps me make sense of my experiences and find meaning in my pain. For example, a butterfly emerging from a cocoon can symbolize transformation and rebirth. Likewise, changing seasons reminds me that change is a natural and necessary part of life.

Spending time in nature can tap into the healing power of the natural world. It helped me find grounding and connection, take time for self-care and reflection, and draw inspiration and meaning from the symbolism and metaphor of the natural world. Our dear planet Earth can be a helpful and supportive presence for those suffering from the restlessness of a broken heart through love.

Three

The Karmic Cycle

Realize that everything connects to everything else.
Leonardo da Vinci

Understanding Karma and its effect on my life has also helped me understand why I was going through heartbreak and pain. This understanding also gave me the insight that I should accept and find the strength to craft a more beautiful and harmonious life, and, most importantly, I can achieve it through my current thoughts, words, and action.

If you are new to Karma, below is a summary to help you understand how to approach your current situation.

The karmic cycle is a concept in Hinduism, Buddhism, and other Eastern religions that describes the cycle of cause and effect that governs our actions and experiences. According to this belief, every action we take, whether good or bad, creates Karma or a "mental footprint" that affects our future experiences.

The karmic cycle is a wheel, with each turn representing a new incarnation or rebirth. Our past actions determine the quality of our current life, and our everyday actions will determine the quality of our future lives. It means that our actions in this life will determine the nature of our experiences in future lives.

The ultimate goal of the karmic cycle is to achieve Moksha, or liberation from the cycle of rebirth and suffering. It can be achieved by accumulating good Karma through good actions such as meditation, acts of kindness, and selfless service, which can help to purify the mind and free it from attachment and desire.

Overall, the karmic cycle is a fundamental concept in Eastern religions and provides a framework for understanding the relationship between our actions and experiences, both in our lives and future lives.

Types of Karma

My actions are my only true belongings. I cannot escape the consequences of my actions. My actions are the ground on which I stand.
  Nhat Hanh

Hinduism and Buddhism have three types of Karma: Sanchita Karma, Prarabdha Karma, and Kriyamana Karma.

Sanchita Karma: This is the accumulated Karma from all of our past lives that still need to be resolved. It represents our "karmic debt" and influences our current and future lives. One can reduce Sanchita Karma through spiritual practices such as meditation, selfless service, and acts of kindness.

Prarabdha Karma: This portion of our Sanchita Karma has ripened and is now being experienced in our current life. Karma has already been "set in motion" and cannot be changed. One can and should experience it with equanimity and detachment.

Kriyamana Karma: This is the Karma created in the present moment through our thoughts, words, and actions. It is the most important type of Karma, as it has the potential to influence our future experiences. Kriyamana Karma can be modified through self-awareness, intention, and mindful action.

Overall, the three types of Karma work together to shape our current experiences and future lives and provide a framework for understanding the relationship between our actions and spiritual evolution.

A bit of karmic math – Earning, and repayment of credits and debts

For most of us, karma and negative emotions obscure the ability to see our own intrinsic nature and the nature of reality. As a result, we clutch onto happiness and suffering as real, and in our unskillful and ignorant actions, we go on sowing the seeds of our next birth. Our actions keep us bound to the continuous cycle of worldly existence, to the endless round of birth and death. So everything is at risk in how we live now at this very moment: How we live now can cost us our entire future.
Sogyal Rinpoche

Karma and mathematics seem like two very different concepts but share some similarities. Both involve the idea of cause and effect, and both operate according to specific laws and principles.

One way to think about the relationship between Karma and mathematics is to use the analogy of a mathematical equation. Just as an equation has two sides that must be balanced to be accurate, Karma involves balancing the effects of our past actions with our actions in the present.

For example, if we have accumulated negative Karma from past actions, we may experience difficulties and challenges in our current life. However, by taking positive actions in the present, we can create positive Karma that will balance the negative Karma and lead to a more positive future.

Similarly, equations must be balanced in mathematics by performing the same operation on both sides. If we add or subtract something from one side, we must do the same to the other to maintain the balance.

In this way, the concepts of Karma and mathematics both involve balance and emphasize the importance of taking responsibility for our actions and understanding the consequences of our choices.

While the relationship between Karma and mathematics may take time to become apparent, both concepts share some fundamental principles. They can offer valuable insights into the nature of cause and effect.

While it's possible to think of good and bad Karma in terms of earning credits and debits, it's important to remember that Karma is a complex and multifaceted concept that cannot be reduced to a simple accounting system.

Karma is not just about accumulating positive or negative outcomes based on our actions but also about the underlying intentions, attitudes, and states of Consciousness that motivate our actions. Additionally, the effects of Karma may only sometimes be immediate or obvious and may play out over the course of multiple lifetimes.

That being said, thinking of good Karma as earning credits and lousy Karma as debits can be a helpful way to conceptualize the concept of Karma and to motivate positive actions. By accumulating positive Karma through good actions, we can "earn" positive outcomes and experiences in the future, while negative Karma may lead to negative consequences.

However, it's essential to approach the concept of Karma with an open-minded perspective and recognize that it is a deeply spiritual and philosophical concept beyond simple cause-and-effect relationships.

When brokenhearted, I was going through intense heartache, and I was relating to the philosophy of Karma in several ways:

Understanding Cause and Effect: The philosophy of Karma teaches that our actions have consequences and that what we put into the world will eventually return to us. When we experience heartbreak, it can be helpful to reflect on the actions and choices that led up to the situation and to consider how we can learn from those experiences and make different choices in the future.

Taking Responsibility: The philosophy of Karma also emphasizes the importance of taking responsibility for our actions and choices. When we experience heartbreak, it can be easy to blame others for our pain, but Karma reminds us that we have the power to choose our actions and choices and are ultimately responsible for our well-being.

Meaning and Purpose: The philosophy of Karma also teaches that everything happens for a reason and that our experiences, even painful ones, can be opportunities for growth and learning. When we experience heartbreak, seeing the purpose or meaning in our pain can be challenging. Still, the philosophy of Karma encourages us to trust that there is a larger plan at work and that our experiences are helping us to grow and evolve as individuals.

Cultivating Compassion and Forgiveness: Finally, the philosophy of Karma emphasizes the importance of developing compassion and forgiveness for ourselves and others. When we experience heartbreak, it can be easy to fall into a cycle of anger, bitterness, and resentment. Still, the philosophy of Karma reminds us that holding onto negative emotions will only perpetuate our suffering. Instead, by cultivating compassion and forgiveness, we can free ourselves from the cycle of pain and move toward healing and growth.

Hence, the philosophy of Karma can provide a framework for understanding and navigating the heartache experienced by someone with a broken heart. By emphasizing cause and effect, taking responsibility, finding meaning and purpose, and cultivating compassion and forgiveness, the philosophy of Karma can help us make sense of our pain, see the lessons in our experiences, and move toward healing and growth.

Suffering = Repaying debts

While dealing with heartbreak and considering the concept of Karma, the question arises: Is suffering repaying one's karmic debts?

In Hinduism and other spiritual traditions that believe in Karma, suffering can be seen as a result of one's past actions or karmic debts. According to this view, every action we take creates a karmic imprint or seed, which will eventually ripen and produce its fruit through experiences or consequences. These consequences may be positive or negative, depending on the nature of the action.

When we experience suffering or difficult circumstances in our current life, it may be seen as a result of negative actions or thoughts we have engaged in during our past lives. The suffering we experience is a way to balance out or repay our karmic debts and create a more positive future for ourselves.

However, Karma is not solely focused on punishment or retribution for past actions. Instead, it emphasizes that our current activities and thoughts can shape our future experiences and create positive change through positive actions and intentions.

So, I adopted this idea in my dealing with suffering and thought that perhaps this suffering I experience is a way I am repaying my karmic debts. They are making me lose accumulated bad Karma. And that I should, from now onwards, focus on creating positive actions and intentions to create a more positive future for myself.

Four

You created this role yourself

Forgetfulness of your real nature is true death; remembrance of it is rebirth.
   Ramana Maharshi

When entangled in despair, I often ask myself, why me? Why do I suffer? Did I create this birth myself? Did I determine who I would be born as?

I found these answers, which I am sharing now with you.

In Hinduism and other spiritual traditions, it is believed that the circumstances of our birth are determined by a combination of our Karma (actions and consequences of those actions) and the cosmic laws of the Universe. Our Karma is the main factor determining our current life situation, including our family, social status, and life experiences.

According to this view, our past actions and thoughts have shaped our current circumstances, including the body we are born into. We may have some influence over our future births based on the actions we take in our current life.

However, it is essential to note that this belief does not necessarily imply that we consciously choose or determine our future births. Instead, it suggests that our current actions and thoughts will determine our future circumstances and experiences in our next life.

Overall, Karma and rebirth emphasize that our actions have consequences and that we are responsible for our choices. By cultivating positive actions and thoughts, we can improve our Karma and create a more positive future for ourselves and others.

How was I born

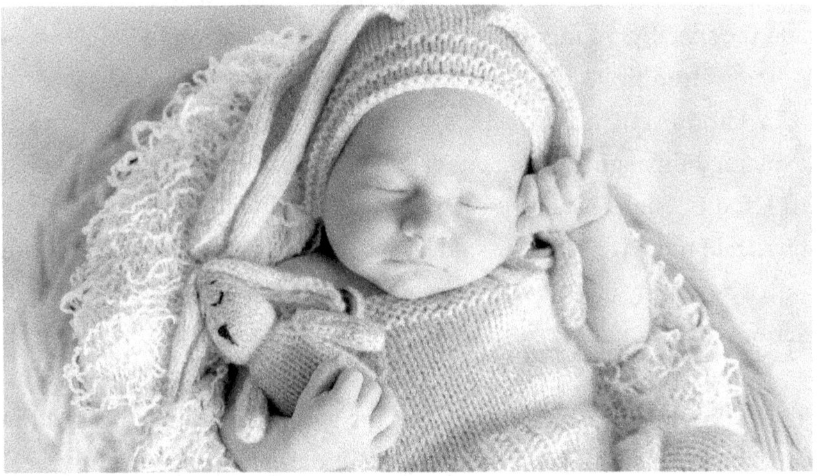

The question of how a soul is born is complex, and the specifics of this process may vary depending on the spiritual or religious tradition.

Some traditions believe that a divine or universal Consciousness creates souls, which are then assigned to a physical body at birth. In other traditions, it is believed that the soul is eternal and exists independent of the physical body and that the body is merely a temporary vessel for the soul during a given incarnation.

In some spiritual or religious traditions, it is believed that the process of birth and the assignment of a soul to a body are influenced by the concept of Karma, which is the idea that our thoughts, words, and actions create a kind of energy that can affect our future experiences and circumstances. In these traditions, it is believed that our past Karma determines the circumstances of our birth and the characteristics of our physical body.

Overall, the question of how a soul is born is complex and multifaceted, and the specifics of this process may vary depending on the spiritual or religious tradition.

In Hinduism, the concept of birth and the creation of a soul is explained through the concept of reincarnation or rebirth. According to Hindu belief, the soul or Atman is eternal and exists beyond the physical body. At death, the soul leaves the physical body and is reborn into a new body based on the previous life's Karma or the accumulated actions and thoughts.

The individual's Karma determines the specific circumstances of the next birth, including the body's social status, family, and physical characteristics. It means that individuals are responsible for their destinies, and the circumstances of their current life result from their actions and thoughts in their previous life.

In Hinduism, the ultimate goal is to break free from the cycle of birth and death and attain Moksha or liberation from the cycle of reincarnation. It is achieved through spiritual practices such as meditation, yoga, and self-realization, which help to purify the soul and break free from the cycle of Karma and rebirth.

Why is the ultimate goal to break free from the cycle of birth and death? What advantages are there?

In Hinduism, the ultimate goal of breaking free from the cycle of birth and death is to achieve Moksha or liberation from the cycle of reincarnation. This liberation is the ultimate goal because it is believed to offer several advantages.

Firstly, liberation from the cycle of birth and death is seen as a release from the suffering and pain inherent in reincarnation. In each life, an individual is subject to the ups and downs of life, including illness, old age, and death, as well as the various forms of suffering that arise from attachment to material possessions and relationships.

Secondly, liberation from the cycle of birth and death is seen as an opportunity to merge with the divine or ultimate reality. The ultimate reality is seen as the source of all existence, and the goal of the spiritual path is to realize one's true nature as a part of this ultimate reality.

Finally, liberation from the cycle of birth and death is seen as a chance to attain complete spiritual freedom and end the cycle of rebirth. It allows the soul to be freed from the constraints of material existence and achieve a state of absolute bliss, knowledge, and unity with the divine.

Overall, breaking free from the cycle of birth and death is seen as the ultimate goal in Hinduism because it offers the opportunity to overcome suffering, merge with the ultimate reality, and attain complete spiritual freedom and bliss.

Now – the current moment when you are alive

Is the present moment all we have to live in the NOW?

Yes, the current moment is all we have to live in the NOW. The present moment is the only moment that truly exists; the past and future are mental constructs we create in our minds. While we can learn from our past experiences and plan for the future, we can only experience and act in the present moment.

Living in the present moment, or the NOW is essential in many spiritual traditions, including Buddhism and mindfulness practices. By being fully present in the current moment, we can develop greater awareness, clarity, and peace. We can also learn to let go of worries about the past or future and focus on what we can control in the present moment.

I learned that practicing mindfulness and living in the NOW has many benefits, including reduced stress and anxiety, improved mental and physical health, increased creativity and productivity, and greater fulfillment and purpose in life.

Practicing mindfulness in everything you do can be a challenge at first, but it can become more natural with practice. Here are some tips for incorporating mindfulness into your daily activities:

1. Start your day mindfully: Before you even get out of bed, take a few deep breaths and set an intention for the day. Focus on being present at the moment and not letting your mind wander to your to-do list or worries.
2. Slow down: In today's fast-paced world, getting caught up in a rush and forgetting to slow down is easy. Try to take a few moments throughout the day to pause, take a deep breath, and tune into your senses.
3. Focus on your senses: When engaged in an activity, focus on your senses. Notice your actions' sights, sounds, smells, tastes, and textures. It can help you stay present in the moment and prevent your mind from wandering.
4. Be fully present: Give them your full attention when you're with others. Put away your phone, turn off the TV, and listen to what they're saying. It can help you build stronger connections and

relationships.

5. Embrace boredom: In today's world, we're often so busy that we don't have time to be bored. But allowing yourself to be bored can be a powerful way to cultivate mindfulness. Instead of filling every moment with activity, try to embrace moments of stillness and let your mind wander.

6. Practice gratitude: When you're doing something, take a moment to appreciate it. Whether you're eating a meal, walking, or spending time with loved ones, focus on what you're grateful for at that moment. It can help cultivate a sense of mindfulness and contentment.

Remember, mindfulness is a practice that takes time and effort to cultivate. Start small and be patient with yourself as you develop your mindfulness practice.

Desires will get you here as many times as you wish

In many spiritual or religious traditions, there is a belief that the accumulation of desires or attachments can lead to suffering and can contribute to the cycle of birth and rebirth. The specifics of this belief may vary depending on the tradition. Still, the general idea is that our desires and attachments can keep us trapped in the material world and prevent us from realizing our true spiritual nature.

For example, in Hinduism and Buddhism, the cycle of birth and rebirth (known as samsara) is driven by the accumulation of Karma generated by our actions and desires. The more we are attached to our desires and the outcomes of our actions, the more Karma we accumulate, and the more likely we will be reborn in future life.

In some traditions, it is believed that the accumulation of desires can also impact our current life, leading to dissatisfaction and suffering. For example, in Buddhism, the Four Noble Truths state that suffering is caused by desire and that the cessation of desire is the path to liberation from suffering.

Overall, the relationship between desires and rebirth is a complex topic, and the specifics of this belief may vary depending on the spiritual or religious tradition. However, many traditions emphasize the importance of cultivating detachment and letting go of our desires to achieve greater spiritual fulfillment and liberation from suffering.

Detachment and letting go of desires are central practices in many spiritual traditions and can be challenging to cultivate. Here are some steps you can take to start cultivating detachment:

1. Recognize the impermanence of all things: Understanding that everything in life is impermanent, including our thoughts, emotions, and experiences, can help us let go of attachment to them. We can see things as they are without trying to hold onto or change them.

2. Observe your thoughts and emotions: Practice observing your thoughts and emotions without judgment or attachment. Instead of identifying with your thoughts and emotions, observe them as they arise and pass away.

3. Practice non-attachment in daily life: Start by practicing non-attachment in small ways, such as letting go of attachments to material possessions or expectations for how things should be. Notice when attachment arises and practice letting go in that moment.

4. Develop a daily meditation practice: Meditation is a powerful tool for cultivating detachment and letting go. Regular meditation allows us to observe our thoughts and emotions without becoming attached.

5. Cultivate gratitude and contentment: Focusing on what we have rather than what we lack can help us cultivate gratitude and contentment, which can, in turn, help us let go of attachment to desires and expectations.

6. Let go of the need for control: Recognize that many things in life are outside our control, and learn to let go of the need to control outcomes. Instead, focus on what is within your control, such as your thoughts and actions.

Remember that cultivating detachment is a lifelong practice that takes time and effort to develop. Be patient with yourself and practice regularly; over time, you will experience greater spiritual fulfillment and liberation from suffering.

Thoughts have substance

Our life is what our thoughts make it.
  Marcus Aurelius

We have already seen in the section on Karma that what we think influences our Karmic account. So, it means that thoughts are powerful. We should pay attention to what we think.

Scientists, philosophers, and spiritual practitioners debate whether thoughts have substance.

From a scientific perspective, thoughts are often considered to be the result of electrical and chemical activity in the brain. While this activity can be measured and observed, it is not generally considered to have substance like physical objects.

However, from a philosophical or spiritual perspective, thoughts having substance may be interpreted differently. Some spiritual or religious traditions believe in the concept of an energetic or spiritual body that is closely connected to the physical body, which our thoughts and emotions can influence. In these traditions, thoughts are seen as having an energetic or spiritual substance that can impact our well-being and the world around us.

Overall, the question of whether thoughts have substance is complex and multifaceted and may be answered differently depending on the context and perspective from which it is approached.

How can thoughts bring a soul back into existence with a body?

From a spiritual perspective, the relationship between thoughts and the existence of a soul with a body is often seen as being influenced by the concept of Karma, which is the idea that our thoughts, words, and actions create a kind of energy that can affect our future experiences and circumstances.

In some spiritual or religious traditions, it is believed that our thoughts can influence the circumstances of our next incarnation. For example, we cultivate positive and compassionate thoughts. In that case, we may be reborn into more favorable circumstances, whereas if we produce harmful thoughts, we may be reborn into less fortunate circumstances.

However, it is essential to note that the relationship between thoughts and the existence of a soul with a body is complex and may be understood differently depending on the spiritual or religious tradition. Additionally, all belief systems may not accept or acknowledge the concept of rebirth or reincarnation.

In any case, my thinking was, if thoughts are so powerful, if I can get on the right stream, the correct current of thought, it will then take me to where I would like to get to for now, in this moment of pain– to healing my broken heart. A positive outlook is a right stream, the proper river, and the right flight to find healing, which paves the way to further growth and self-development.

What are you here to do

You are not here merely to make a living. You are here in order to enable the world to live more amply, with greater vision, and with a finer spirit of hope and achievement. You are here to enrich the world, and you impoverish yourself if you forget the errand.
Woodrow Wilson

What is the objective of our birth?

The aim of our birth is a question that many philosophical and spiritual traditions have pondered. In Hinduism, the ultimate aim of human birth is to achieve Moksha, which is liberation from the cycle of birth and death (samsara) and the attainment of oneness with the divine.

In other spiritual traditions, such as Buddhism, the objective of human birth may be seen as achieving enlightenment or Nirvana, which involves transcending the ego-self and attaining peace, wisdom, and compassion.

Ultimately, the objective of human birth may be a deeply personal and subjective question and can vary depending on one's beliefs, values, and experiences.

In a more general sense, the objective of human birth is finding meaning and purpose in life, cultivating positive relationships and experiences, and contributing to the well-being of others and the world around us. The more we work towards these goals, the more fulfilled we feel in this life, despite the heartbreaks we may have to go through.

Five

The Cycle of Life

L ife is like riding a bicycle. To keep your balance, you must keep moving.
Albert Einstein

Just like I considered the vast space, galaxies, and universes, thinking about the cycle of life provided me with the realization that things change. Nothing ever stays the same, and I can only move forward. Having a positive mindset toward this movement will be helpful for me to establish a good foundation for my body, mind, and soul.

Below are the key points which I meditated on while processing my heartache, and letting these thoughts cleanse me and power me forward.

The cycle of life refers to the process of birth, growth, decline, and death that all living beings experience. It is a fundamental aspect of the natural world, characterized by constant energy and change.

In many spiritual and philosophical traditions, the cycle of life is seen as a reflection of the larger cycles of nature and the cosmos. It is a circle or wheel, with each stage of life representing a different point on the cycle.

The cycle of life typically begins with birth or creation, followed by growth and development. As the being matures, it reaches a peak of strength and vitality before starting to decline and eventually experiencing death. After death, the being may be reborn or reabsorbed into the larger cycle of existence, beginning the process anew.

The cycle of life is often associated with themes of impermanence, transformation, and renewal and is viewed as a reminder of the interconnectedness and interdependence of all things. In many spiritual traditions, the cycle of life is seen as an opportunity for growth, learning, and spiritual evolution, as beings move through the various stages of life and experience the many challenges and joys that come with each step.

Six

The foundation of life — A big fire of Consciousness with little sparks of soul

As innumerable sparks emanate from a fire, all the jīvas with their particular characteristics emanate from the Paramātma, along with the gods, planets, and animate and inanimate beings. (Bṛhad-āraṇyaka Upaniṣad 2.1.20)

Every time I encounter heartbreak, I find solace in the fact that everything is connected and will return to the foundation, the big Fire of Super Consciousness, God. We, the souls, are the sparks of that Fire and will eventually merge into Him.

The foundation of life can be understood in several different ways, depending on one's perspective and worldview. Here are a few possible interpretations:

Biological foundation: From a scientific perspective, the foundation of life is the set of processes and structures that make it possible for living organisms to survive, reproduce, and evolve. It includes things like cellular metabolism, DNA replication, and genetic variation.

Spiritual foundation: From a spiritual or religious perspective, the foundation of life is the divine or transcendent force that imbues all living things with Consciousness, purpose, and meaning. One can understand it in terms of a particular deity, universal life force, or other spiritual concepts.

Philosophical foundation: From a philosophical perspective, the foundation of life is the fundamental principles or values that underlie human existence and guide our actions and choices. It might include concepts like love, justice, compassion, or the pursuit of knowledge and truth.

Cosmic foundation: From a cosmological perspective, the foundation of life is the more extensive physical and metaphysical structures that make life possible in the Universe, such as the laws of physics, the formation of stars and planets, and the emergence of complex systems and patterns.

Overall, the foundation of life is a complex and multifaceted concept from many different angles. At its core, however, it is a reminder of the wonder and mystery of existence and the many interconnected factors that make life possible.

In many spiritual or religious traditions, humans and living beings are seen as souls or consciousnesses that inhabit physical bodies. This concept's specific beliefs and interpretations may vary depending on the tradition or culture. Still, the general idea is that the soul or Consciousness is eternal and transcends the physical body.

For example, in Hinduism, the concept of the Atman or soul is central to the belief system. The belief is that every living has an eternal and unchanging soul that reincarnates in different physical bodies over the course of many lifetimes. Similarly, Buddhism sees the self or ego as an illusion. The spiritual practice aims to realize the soul's true nature or Consciousness and achieve liberation from the cycle of birth and death.

In other spiritual or religious traditions, the concept of the soul is interpreted differently. For example, in Christianity, the soul is often seen as a unique aspect of human beings that God creates and survives after death, but there may not be a belief in reincarnation.

Overall, the concept of the soul or Consciousness as a separate entity from the physical body is a common theme in many spiritual or religious traditions and is often associated with the idea that there is a deeper, more meaningful dimension to existence beyond the material world.

Hence, meditating on the foundation of life will imbue one with a sense of connectedness and stability. Though there are many waves on the surface, at the bottom of the ocean foundation, there's stillness, depth, strength, and life.

Seven

*How can one heal oneself from a heart
broken by love?*

There is no remedy for love but to love more.
Henry David Thoreau

So far, I have been sharing viewpoints, perspectives, thoughts, considerations, and arguments about how I attempted to heal my broken heart. Healing from a heart broken by love is a complex and multifaceted process that takes time and could also involve various strategies and approaches, like the ones I outlined in this book. Below are some ideas of how you can begin to heal yourself from heartbreak through love:

Practice self-care: Taking good care of yourself physically, emotionally, and mentally is vital for healing from heartbreak. It may involve activities such as exercise, eating healthy food, getting enough sleep, and engaging in activities that bring you joy and relaxation.

Seek support: It can be helpful to reach out to friends, family members, or a therapist during this difficult time. Having someone to talk to and share your feelings with can provide comfort and help you to process your emotions.

Cultivate self-awareness: Pay attention to your thoughts and emotions, and identify any patterns or beliefs contributing to your heartbreak. You can make positive changes in your life and relationships by developing self-awareness.

Practice mindfulness: Developing mindfulness, such as meditation or deep breathing exercises, can help to calm your mind and reduce stress and anxiety. It can be beneficial during times of emotional upheaval.

Explore spirituality: Spiritual practices and beliefs can provide comfort and connection during difficult times. It may involve meditation, prayer, or engaging in a spiritual community.

Focus on positive actions: Rather than dwelling on past pain, focus on taking positive steps in the present. It may involve setting goals, engaging in activities that bring you joy, and cultivating gratitude for the blessings in your life.

From experience, I have found that healing from heartbreak through love is a process that takes time and effort. By practicing self-care, seeking support, cultivating self-awareness, practicing mindfulness, exploring spirituality, and focusing on positive actions, you can begin to move forward and heal from the pain of the past.

II

Hope for a brighter future

Eight

How I found my soulmate

You know you're in love when you can't fall asleep because reality is finally better than your dreams."- **Dr. Seuss**

Finding a life partner or soul mate can be challenging, especially if you suffer from a broken heart. Here are some suggestions that may help you in your search:

1. Take time to heal: Before you start looking for a new relationship, it's essential to give yourself time to heal and process your emotions. Take the time you need to focus on yourself and your well-being.
2. Reflect on what you want in a partner: Reflect on your past relationships and what you learned from them. Consider what qualities are important to you in a partner and what you want in a relationship.
3. Be open to new experiences: Try new things and be open to meeting new people. It can broaden your social circle and increase your chances of meeting someone who is a good match for you.
4. Connect with like-minded people: Join groups or organizations that align with your interests and values. It can help you to connect with people who share your passions and values.
5. Use online dating platforms: Online dating can be a helpful tool for meeting new people. Choose a reputable platform that suits your needs and preferences, and be clear about what you're looking for in your profile.
6. Practice good communication: When you start dating, practice good communication skills. Be clear and honest about your feelings and expectations, and listen actively to your partner.

Finding a life partner or soul mate can be challenging and may take time. Focus on taking good care of yourself, being open to new experiences, and trusting that the right person will come into your life when the time is right.

The Soulmate Manifesting Mantra

I followed my path to finding my soulmate by chanting this mantra. It is a well-known and old mantra, but I came across it when I bought and read the book Healing Mantras by Ashley-Farrand, Thomas.

For a woman seeking her soulmate, in Sanskrit, the manta is **Sat Patim Dehi Parameshwara**.

The English translation is Dear God; please grant me a noble, virtuous, and truthful man.

Sat = Truth

Patim = Spouse, Man, Husband, Partner

Dehi = to give

Parameshwara = Almighty God

For a man seeking his wife, replace the word Patim with Patni. In

Sanskrit, Patni means wife.

The mantra is **Sat Patni Dehi Parameshwara**.

Sat = Truth

Patni = Wife

Dehi = to give

Parameshwara = Almighty God

How I performed the mantra chanting-

1. The first step I undertook was to write down in a notebook the kind of man I wanted in my life – his qualities (loving, kind, trustworthy, patient, wants to have a family, etc., spiritual) and character (good, morally upright, truthful, etc.).

2. Every morning, as soon as I woke up, even when lying in bed, I say a short prayer to God (Nature, Higher Self, Higher Consciousness, along the lines of -

Dear God, thank you for guarding me when I was asleep and allowing me to wake up this morning. Please bless my family and friends, and be with me throughout the day.

You know I am seeking my soul mate; please bless my efforts and help me find him.

He should be a man of such and such qualities and character. Here, I was mentally listing the things I had written down.

Then I chanted the mantra 108 times. Even though I was lying in bed, I used my fingers and toes to keep count.

To end the prayer, I always said, "Let there be sufficient rain so that all people, animals, and plants on this earth may live well.

3. I was reading the details of the kind of person I wanted that I had written down at least once a day – mainly in the afternoons.

4. Before I went to bed, I said a short prayer to God every night.

Dear God, thank you for being with me throughout the day. Today, I did these things well, and I could have done these things differently. Please bless my family and friends and be with me through the night.

You know that I am looking for my soul mate. Please bless my efforts and help me find him. He should be a man of such and such qualities and character. Here, I was mentally listing the things I had written down.

Then I chanted the mantra 108 times.

I had performed this prayer quite intensely for at least 40 days and continued for another three months or so. I was chanting this mantra for four and a half months.

Today, this mantra has several beautiful musical renderings on YouTube, which one can listen to throughout the day.

It is optional to chant this mantra in Hindi. One could use English or any other language you prefer. Please know the meaning of your chant or prayer. God understands no matter what language.

Amplification of prayers through fasting

There are plenty of books available which talk about the benefits of fasting. One of the benefits is that your prayers are amplified and deeper, reflecting the earnest nature of your appeal.

I chose Monday as my fasting day, as the God I was praying to was the ancient Lord Shiva, the Adiyogi. Monday is supposed to be a special day for remembering Him. I started a vow to fast in the mornings for 21 Mondays. It means I did not take breakfast and ate just after noon on Mondays.

A miracle happens

It happened at the end of my nearly four-and-a-half months of fasting and chanting. I met my husband.

I knew he was the one, and he, too, "recognized" me.

Since then, we have been together and living a harmonious life by the grace of God.

And as a mark of gratitude, I continue my Monday fasting, and my husband has joined me on these fasts.

It also helps to keep my weight in check!

Nine

In closing

"Being deeply loved by someone gives you strength, while loving someone deeply gives you courage." — **Lao Tzu**

As we come to the end of this book, it's clear that the journey of healing a broken heart is complex. We can use many tools, techniques, and philosophies to help us move through the pain and find a sense of peace and wholeness once again. But ultimately, the path to healing is personal, and what works for one person may not work for another.

However, some common threads run through all the approaches we've explored. Mindfulness, for example, is a powerful tool for cultivating awareness and presence in our lives, helping us to break free from negative thought patterns and connect with our inner selves. By bringing mindfulness into our everyday activities, we can deepen our connection to the present moment and learn to let go of our worries and anxieties. It is a path that requires us to continually examine our thoughts, beliefs, and actions and question the stories we tell ourselves about who we are and what we need to be happy.

Similarly, detachment and letting go can help us find greater spiritual fulfillment and liberation from suffering. By learning to accept what is and detach ourselves from our desires and expectations, we can free ourselves from the pain of disappointment and create space for joy and peace to enter our lives by opening ourselves up to the beauty and abundance of the present moment.

Of course, these practices are not easy, and there will be times when we stumble or fall back into old patterns. But the key is to keep going and showing up for ourselves and our healing. Remember that healing is not a destination but a journey and that each step we take, no matter how small, brings us closer to wholeness.

So, as you continue healing your heart, remember to be kind to yourself, take time for self-care and self-compassion, and lean on the support of loved ones and the wisdom of spiritual teachings.

In my experience, praying and chanting with faith can manifest one's, soul mate. If you are willing to go through the efforts, be patient, be focused, and be mindful, the big expansive Universe will answer your prayers, and you will find what you seek.

May you find peace, joy, and love on your journey and emerge from this experience stronger, wiser, and more whole than ever before.

A kind request

I would be thrilled to hear from you with your questions or comments. My email address is mina.soundar@gmail.com.

If you found this book helpful, please leave positive feedback. It will be helpful for me to continue writing books like this to provide support to those who might be in need.

Please also check out my book, Fertility Magic, where I narrate how I naturally conceived my child at 45.